IF IT HEALS AT ALL

Ali Black

Cover & interior design: Daniel Krawiec
Cover photograph: "That's that Tunnel" by Donald Black, Jr.
(donaldblackjr.com)

ISBN 978-0-936481-42-5

Jacar Press
6617 Deerview Trail
Durham, NC 27712
www.jacarpress.com

For Zelma & Johnny B.

CONTENTS

2 | KINSMAN

I

6 | INFLAMMATION

7 | REMEMBERING SMOKE

9 | IF YOU WOULD'VE MET MY MOTHER

10 | AS SOON AS THEY DIAGNOSED ME I TEXTED MY GIRL IN ATLANTA

11 | BAD NURSE

12 | CODE YELLOW

13 | AFTER I WAS DONE BEING DEPRESSED I CALLED BENA

14 | B-SIDE PERFORMANCE, 2007

15 | THE WOMEN IN MY FAMILY ALL CLEAN THE SAME

16 | I AM QUEEN OF THE FOLD

II

18 | I WORE AN "I LOVE SHARON REED" T-SHIRT ON MY 30TH BIRTHDAY AND GOT BEAT UP & ARRESTED BY THE CLEVELAND POLICE

19 | IN BETWEEN TRYING TO SURVIVE

20 | DOUBLE DARE

21 | HOW TO GO TAGGING WHEN IN LOVE

22 | HOW A POEM & A WEDDING SAVED MY LIFE

23 | THE WAYS YOU LOVE MY HAIR

24 | BRA LOG, 2020

25 | SKATE

26 | RIDING THE 14

28 | PRETTY RIVER POEM

29 | LATE SHIFT AT THE TOUCH OF ITALY

30 | SHE ASKED ME HOW TO KNOW IF SHE IS THE SIDE CHICK

31 | SIGNIFICANCE

32 | I ALWAYS THOUGHT LADY GAGA HAD LUPUS

33 | THE MOMENTS WE WOULD'VE SHARED WITH MY FATHER

35 | Acknowledgements

"So much of life is pain and sorrow and wilful ignorance and violence, and pushing back against that tide takes so much effort, so much steady fight. It's tiring."

— Jesmyn Ward

KINSMAN

the day after the baby is killed
by a gunshot wound to the chest

you still have to ride behind
death's bloodred breath.

you still have to picture
the baby in the car trying

to grab the bullet as if it were
a glossy sweet thing.

you do not want to imagine
the pitch of the baby's wail.

you do not want to see the women
walking with bright white Save-A-Lot

bags wrapped around their wrists.
you do not want to see the man

at the RTA bus stop swatting at a bee.
you do not want to see

anyone trying to hurt anything.
you do not want to face

the red lights, the teddy bear memorials,
the trash, the raggedy strollers, the slow

slow walk of the low-down folks.
you do not want to ride by

the hand-painted *Casino Trip!* sign
stapled high on a pole like a goal.

you do not want to hear the radio
scroll through tragedy and woe.

you hear the beginning of the word
Oregon and you know the next

stories will be about more shootings.
you think about the baby killed by the bullet.

I

INFLAMMATION

Her lungs were clouded too. So, by this time, my mama was too tired to tell me I should've never had my Black ass outside in the dead of a Cleveland winter running around without a coat on. And so, there we were, two more women worried & ill Black bodies waiting for another diagnosis. If I believed in making up memories to forgive myself, I'd write this poem smooth into a lie. I'd tell y'all I told my mama *I love you* so many times the doctor had to remind me I wasn't dying, not for real I wasn't. I mean, the pop-off-at-anything side of me had itself halfway in the grave mainly cuz it was scaring my mama too much, had her calling me manic. And like all Black girls, I was tired of people mistaking my mouth as a disorder. Anyway, I'd turn this poem into a dream and in the dream my mama would be the doctor, and to heal me, all she'd do is give me a kiss, and I'd piss out the fluid in my lungs because how else does a Black girl survive a deadly virus?

REMEMBERING SMOKE

I. Morning Cigarette

I knew she would smoke forever.

By the time I was in high school she was lighting up in bed
before she even turned on the news.

I'd hear the cough, cough, cough, cough
cut through her words like a rude interruption.

"Rise and shine," she always tried to say.

II. Stress

She was pissed if she smoked without an ashtray.
Ashes in the dishwater affirmed her anger.

She'd be dicing an onion for potato salad
and somebody would call to smother her with gossip.

"People get on my last nerve," she'd say.

Then, she'd lean over the sink, Viceroy in hand,
and I'd watch the ashes fall into the soapy water.

III. Secondhand Smoke

On our quick trips to Mother Dear's house
my brother and I exaggerated our coughs like class clowns.

My mother smoked one cigarette for every two songs.

We hated the cigarette smoke.
We'd cough and cough and pretend to choke.

She'd crack the windows.
For two puffs, she made herself into a small woman
stretching up to kiss some tall and handsome man.
Then she'd blow the smoke out the window.

We'd still cough and complain and she'd simply say

"I know."
"I know."

IV. Quitting

She tried everything to stop smoking:
the patch, peppermints, and prayer.

I prayed too.
Dear God, please help her quit.

At the grocery store I was in charge of scooping
the red and white candies into produce bags.

She taught me to lick my thumb to split the bag open.
"Make it easy," she'd say.

Some evenings we'd take a walk to Euclid Creek.
She'd get so winded she could barely speak.

V. Routine

She did everything with a cigarette dangling between her fingers.
At night I studied her while she rolled her hair.

She'd come to the part where a woman raises her arms
above her head to stretch the hair before the roll,
and I would see the cigarette *still* hanging on like a tight, tight curl.

IF YOU WOULD'VE MET MY MOTHER

She would call you
every Sunday morning

to check on me.
She'd ask you large questions

like how well I'm sleeping
& if my hair is shedding.

She'd love the man in you
knowing I'm safe

with someone who keeps
his cool around cops.

She'd stretch out your name
& play it straight

in the Pick 3.
She'd gamble on you alright.

And you'd be the one
to make her hit.

You'd tell her you
dreamed about a lion

& she'd look it up
in the dream book

& play the number backwards,
box it for three days in row.

AS SOON AS THEY DIAGNOSED ME
I TEXTED MY GIRL IN ATLANTA

Because I believe my friends more than I believe
these sneaky-ass doctors. Plus, she Black, she smart, she fine,
she run, she cook & she pushed her caring, Black ass to become an army nurse.
She the one who told me lupus was an autoimmune disease.
She the one who told me it had a nickname & that's the only reason
I started dreaming about wolf bites.
Dr. Sunshine let the long & boastful term, systemic lupus erythematosus,
settle on his lips like it was a joint he was about to light up
& love. *Another Black girl down,* I pictured his swirl of smoke saying.
I could've punched that fool in his face
because I was convinced he injected me on some
now-you-got-lupus type shit.
When I called my mother, she got so mad
she blamed everything on my father's side.
I laughed like something was funny.

BAD NURSE

The nurse called my doctor
after she saw me writing

the opening lines of Psalm 23
on my forearm.

She knew a Black woman
writing on her own skin meant

the whole world could start again.
And then, who would die from chronic disease?

And then, who would fill the graves?
And then, what would be the point of doctors?

But say the world started again
without Black women

Where would white women get their style?
And who would they disrupt in Target?

And who would they call the police on?
And who would they smother with their privilege?

And who would dust their furniture?
And who would they lie on?

And who would their husbands kill?
And whose children would they damage?

And whose bodies would they bump?
And whose bodies would they mock?

And whose bodies would they burn?
And whose bodies would they shoot?

And whose bodies would they ignore?
And whose bodies would they take?

And whose call lights would they ignore?

CODE YELLOW

I was only gone for like five minutes before they called a code yellow on me.
I know my team of doctors thought I was tryna dip, but I was only tryna see
if I could find me a Polish Boy or a can of peach pop. And let's be honest,
if a Black woman keeps waking up to white men in white coats, how long
you think she gone lay there before she decides to get up and run? The PA
system said, a Black female, wearing pink- and maroon-colored pajamas, was
missing. And I swear to you, the only thing I can think about now is how right
they were. It's like damn, I really was missing.

AFTER I WAS DONE BEING DEPRESSED
I CALLED BENA

& she came over & told me I got a little too skinny & my hair looked a little funny & then we laughed until she played The Fray's "How to Save a Life" & then she told me how many times she played that song for me on her way to the job she hated & that's how fast Black girls catch up & forgive each other & that's actually how I started listening to white boy bands & how I got hip to Chrisette Michele. The next day I went to a park all the way in Chagrin Falls & let every song from Chrisette's *I Am* album play three times before I went on to the next song & every day after that I took my time taking in everything I ever loved.

B-SIDE PERFORMANCE, 2007

After my depression, I was on some different shit. I remember this one day I stayed in Dillard's for hours cuz I was trying to find something sexy to perform my poems in. I decided on this wine-colored halter bra dress that I knew would snatch them B-Side niggas' attention cuz most of them niggas be there for the pussy, not the poetry. I knew my dress would pull them in. Before the show, I called my girls to be witnesses. Ronnie was hungry so we stopped at Eaton Place & had dinner at Bravo where this white man told me I was so gorgeous there was no way he could let us pay for our meals. Once we got in my car I had Bena play Kanye's *Graduation* just so I could hear him say, *Welcome to the good life.* I was 27 and that night, B-Side was lit, meaning I had to debo my way on stage cuz half the niggas trying to perform don't believe in ladies first. For real, when the host says, *The mic is open,* niggas bum-rush the stage like the mic might be the only thing keeping all of us alive.

THE WOMEN IN MY FAMILY ALL CLEAN THE SAME
— after Russell Atkins

they swear it'll bring back the dead / they mix water, sunlight & white vinegar
to clean their mirrors / they use newspaper to wipe their glass tables / they sprinkle baking soda on
their pillows / they clean before the streetlights come on / they iron their bedsheets
on the highest setting / they call it spirit cleansing / they scrub their toilets & tubs with flathead
toothbrushes / they promise it sharpens your memory / they wipe down their walls once a week /
they splash a pinch of apple cider vinegar in their laundry / they gargle with peroxide & salt
to whiten their teeth / they insist it brings in money / they sweep with wooden brooms / they hand-
wash their bras & panties / they keep their cleaning supplies in special dark corners / they wash
their floors with string mops / they polish their furniture with elbow grease / they train their
children to "throw that mess away" / they blast Anita Baker / they believe
filth causes headaches / they never ever wear gloves

I AM QUEEN OF THE FOLD

The woman next to me
begins folding her load
of pink and white towels.

She don't even separate
the pink pile from the white one.

She ain't got nothin' on my mother.

My mother folded towels like they had somewhere special to be.
She'd lay them flat, smooth them out,
then fold them into thirds.

I learned from my mother
to match all of her grace

and now, in this Laundromat,
I am queen of the fold.

II

I WORE AN "I LOVE SHARON REED" T-SHIRT ON MY 30TH BIRTHDAY AND GOT BEAT UP & ARRESTED BY THE CLEVELAND POLICE

whenever I tell this story my wife says she could've never been the girl who was with us that the cop body-slammed on the hood of his car because she was trying to record a part of our history that now rattles us anytime we try to celebrate. I know my wife pictures herself hurting the cop's body before he could ever try and lay a hand on hers, but that type of dreaming only exists when you can no longer celebrate. I tell her how my words meant nothing to the cop who twisted my nose after I told him my uncle wore blue too as if colors ever united any of us. I let her know one of the smartest niggas with us took off his "I Love Sharon Reed" shirt and bounced as if he remembered his mother telling him to never ride four deep in a car or otherwise become a target by kicking it with a group of thirty niggas on W. 6th Street in downtown Cleveland after LeBron James makes his decision to leave a city that calls you and your friends a gang because you are all dressed in the same T-shirt.

IN BETWEEN TRYING TO SURVIVE

I be up in my wife's office taking pictures of her vision board. She got quotes by Ralph Ellison telling us the individual is the minority, so it looks like we're all alone after all. I got Lucille Clifton in my bones. She already told me to celebrate every time something tries to kill me and fails. So, here I am skating in the living room on Valentine's Day while my wife dances in front of me in her Vans, her hair as big as the song's bass. You can't kill a Black man, not for real. Listen, Emmett Till ain't never going away. I don't care what you say. Being Black ain't nothing but a crazy alley-oop. We hold each other down despite what you've heard. There's no such thing as spare time in my world. But when I am still I breathe long and light one up for everything that I am. The first thing I think about in the morning is success, art, love & my mama. Everything ain't always about white people, so I wear a hoodie every day. My life is a practice. I eat oatmeal for breakfast. My wife leads little Black girls after school. She watches them bond over hot chips. They walk each other home, stretch in the summer & listen to Beyoncé's Pandora. All their time together is the definition of energy & good times. Sometimes I pop wheelies to feel a balance. All my clothes are black. I love how I live. I sketch dark bodies on my iPad at night. None of my days feel the same. I'm on to the next big thing. My garage is a studio. I made it that way. My black is a heartbeat. I have skin like the ocean. Don't you dare pity me. I never eat your cheese. No need to look me up. I am everywhere. I need more poems like this. Everybody has a voice so what do you mean by voiceless? Don't grin if you can't say hello. I used to burn linen candles. It's not too late to pay me. One photograph is never enough. I got a sharp eye and steady hands. It all makes sense why I stopped tryna get brush waves a long time ago. I pay attention to everything. I don't ever stop. My swag could save a sick thing. When I create art a flower blooms. I'm with the have-nots. We eat catfish, fries, and coleslaw on hot summer days.

DOUBLE DARE

in our version we ditched the trivia questions
& went straight for the physical challenge.
we knew back then how meaningful it was to create
because we knew how fast the world would
weaken our imaginations once it began.
we used washcloths as flags & hid them under mattresses.
we slid down stair railings.
we built booby traps.
we did not call ourselves the red or blue team.
it was simply me & my cousin against my brother.
we were good at making up dangerous games.
in one, we tripped each other to see who could avoid the fall.
in another, we popped each other with warm wet towels.
we wrestled, imitating our favorite Hulk Hogan move.
our love for innocent violence began early.
we never knew how it would haunt us.

HOW TO GO TAGGING WHEN IN LOVE

Give your girl a nickname.

Call her Wildflower and watch her write it a thousand ways.

See her sketch the first *l* as a daisy and fall in love again.

Wear Timberlands and hoodies.

Get ready for the mud.

Pack a silver Durango with spray paint and stencils.

Blast some Kanye on the way.

Search for boarded-up buildings in the "hood."

Make sure your girl is safe.

Show her how to jump out the car and hop a fence.

Tell her to move fast.

Get her inspired.

If she holds back ask her if she wants to go back home.

When she says no tell her you are nervous too.

Pull up, hop out
grab the paint
watch her tag her name.

HOW A POEM & A WEDDING SAVED MY LIFE

So look, if that poem had never came as a hum in my ear,
I'd still be in my corner apartment tallying all the times the world did me dirty.

Poem came busting in like my mama sent it.

Poem came with some kind of god in it.

Poem said,
It is so in you.
I'ma shake the fear out you.
But you better beat the devil till he turn black & blue.

Poem had me calling Bena to see if she'd stop by even though
I had allowed the world to snatch a year away from us.

Poem had me power walking with ankle weights on all up and down Chagrin
just in case the world tried to act like it wanted some more.

Poem lifted me up in one stanza,
as if the stanza was an arm
and the arm was covered in a sleeve
and the sleeve was made up of all my brother's tattoos,
meaning all his dead friends was there to help him lift & pull.

Poem was in straight beast mode.

And look, thank god Black girls do in fact get married.
If not, my girl Ronnie may have never needed the poet in me.

And thank god she chose burnt orange & gold for her colors.
Otherwise, I would've never known how it feels to be a walking sunset.

THE WAYS YOU LOVE MY HAIR

Donald: I am listening.

Most mornings my hair is a mess.
You tell me it is beautiful.

You like it massive and wild.
You call it untamed
and swat at my hands
as I try to control it.

*

I pull my hair up into a high bun
five out of seven days for you.

You like it this way:
Hair up, face available.

*

You want to photograph me
with my hair in thick plaits.

So begins the braiding.

BRA LOG, 2020

Tonight—I take
my bra off and Donald
takes me to the mirror.
He points to all the dark
marks from my bra and calls
it all bullshit. He reminds
me that I wear my bra
too tight, but he forgets
that I am too afraid
to loosen the straps
because I fear my breasts
will shift out of place
or droop like the letter
j or sag like a load of
heavy clothes. But I am
so against bruises. They
make me nervous. They
scare me more than
insecurity because I do not
want to be flawed, which
honestly, is the root of
insecurity.
I have believed
some of what they've
taught me about beauty,
and tonight I recognize
that this ain't about
a bra being too tight.
This is about learning
insecurity is the
worst kind of bruise.

SKATE

My love is roller-skating in our house again.

I roll my eyes as he scuffs our hardwood floors,
but I still bob my head to "Black Superman."

I can't lie.
He looks so good when he shuffles.
He turns and twists and glides
while I try to hide my smile.

Why should I worry about the scuffs
when he is busy moving to the groove?

RIDING THE 14

— after Russell Atkins

Lil' homie warns me
about riding the 14,
says his mama used
to drive that route
& she saw all kinds
of things & I tell him
that's perfect because
I'm tryna write a poem
about riding the bus
& I want to see all kinds
of things even things
a woman shouldn't see.
But when I board,
way before theft's hour,
the bus is quiet & empty
as a box. I take a seat
in back behind a boy
in a pink & purple fatigue
do-rag. I stare at the nosy
single braid poking out
of his do-rag as if it wants
to say hello. When we ride
pass 144th I can't help
but think about the four new
bodies they found in a bando
& then two young girls board
the bus. One girl is rockin'
a small afro & a pair of bamboo
earrings with the word "Baddie"
sliced through the center. She
carries a copy of *The Autobiography*
of Assata Shakur & now everything
feels alright & by the time
I take my eyes off her & the book

at least a half dozen students
have boarded & everybody seems
to possess something purple—a pair
of headphones, a hoodie or a jacket.
The students sit still, glued
to their phones, & I think about
my lil' homie's warning & realize
I'm on at the wrong hour.

PRETTY RIVER POEM

Why the day after we ride to the Flats
they find a dead man's
body in the Cuyahoga River?
And of course when we at the river
to write a pretty river poem
a white woman sitting on the boardwalk
want us to tell her where the weed at.
She try to offer us beer
but we there for the river
and ask her to back up
but she persistent like the river.
She got on all blue & grey
so she look like the river.
She kinda move like the river.
She even got a story like the river.

LATE SHIFT AT THE TOUCH OF ITALY
— after Russell Atkins

by now the men have ordered
their third round of Rémy
& I see the "lick her" in their eyes
they stare, then wink, then tip
slim, fine woman slides a bill
into the smart jukebox
for some Meg Thee Stallion

it is a hot girl summer
& I am drained from these sons
but dedicated to this money
me with my promoted bust
I pour beer after beer
they beg me to dance
I twerk a bit, smirk a bit

I will not old
I will not woe

I will not old
I will not woe

SHE ASKED ME HOW TO KNOW
IF SHE IS THE SIDE CHICK

I'm thinking to myself, *do I look like I know?*
but then I remembered baby girl needed answers
cuz even though she had Summer Walker on repeat,
I know all the answers to love don't show up in music.
so, I'm like, *girl . . . you just know.* but she needed more.
so first, I stretched my mouth and roared for her.
then I started wishing how I could sing my mama
back to life cuz then I could just go get her
off the couch, interrupt her lottery watching
& tell her to put on her deepest shade of red lipstick
cuz baby girl gone have to see mama's lips when
mama tell her, *baby girl, you the side chick when you gotta ask.*

SIGNIFICANCE

My mother was named by a young girl
who asked if they could share names.

Her name was Zelma Mae.

I imagine her long and lean like my mother.
Maybe she, too, painted her nails a bright & brilliant red
& wore her hair short with medium curls.

Most likely she was good at math and could divide things with ease.
I bet she counted every cigarette puff & chew,
took long & calming baths,
& maybe she, too, covered her hair with blue silk every night.

Perhaps she ate catfish and spaghetti every Friday,
played Anita Baker's *Rapture*
& drank her Pepsi from a can.

If she was anything like my mother she played the lottery
and wrote her numbers on the back of bills.

Certainly, she was a woman worth meeting.

I ALWAYS THOUGHT LADY GAGA HAD LUPUS

and for a long time I thought I'd write her a letter and she'd donate her 24-karat gold wheelchair to me for my stiff joints but today I'm finding out that Gaga doesn't even have lupus she has synovitis and it's actually Toni Braxton who has lupus and in 2008 she collapsed on stage in Vegas and I'm like how did I miss this Toni is my girl I remember all them car rides when my mother played the hell out of Toni's debut album in '93 I was only 13 and singing them love songs as if I knew what my mama was going through and if somebody made a bet with me today to try and figure out which song from that album was my mother's favorite I'd put everything I have on "Love Shoulda Brought You Home" and now I'm spending most of my time tryna place a face to the you my mama coulda been singing to cuz in '93 she'd already split from my dad and I just can't picture my father cheating and that being the reason she divorced him

THE MOMENTS WE WOULD'VE SHARED
WITH MY FATHER

For you, my father would've
fried the okra with peanut oil.

He'd call you *son*
and y'all would be

down south
drinkin' Rémy Martin.

We'd all go fishing and my father
would bait the hook with a worm.

In a cold and empty basement,
he'd show you how to

kill a rat with a shovel.
Every moment would be

a lesson on
survival.

Acknowledgements

Thank you to the editors of the following publications, in which these poems first appeared:

Academy of American Poets: "Kinsman"
December: "If You Would've Met My Mother"
jubilat: "The Women in My Family All Clean the Same"
One: "Remembering Smoke"

Much gratitude to Jaki Shelton Green for selecting this book for the New Voices series.

Thank you, Patricia Spears Jones, for your incredible mentorship and guidance. I appreciate you for spending so much time with me and my work.

Thank you to the staff at Jacar Press for giving this book a home outside of my Moleskine journals. It feels good here and I appreciate all the care and attention you all gave to this book.

Thank you Na-Te' Sturdivant for always asking me to read you one of my poems. We were working these poems into beauty and you didn't even know it. Thank you for taking deep breaths and smiling wide after every poem. You were secretly telling me the work was strong, which ultimately encouraged me to keep going.

Thank you to my parents, Zelma and Johnny B., for always telling me you loved me. I carry your love and memory with me at all times—it is the key to everything I write.

Thank you to my brother, John, for always being proud of me—it has instilled a healthy work ethic in me. Thank you to the rest of my family and friends for always telling the people in your worlds that I am a writer—it has made me believe in myself more and more.

Thank you to every reader of this book—it belongs to all of us now.

And finally, thank you to my husband, Donald, for making me get honest in my work—it unlocked everything. You are the sharpest teacher, listener, and friend I've ever had. Thank you for loving me.

Ali Black is a writer from Cleveland, Ohio. Ali is a current graduate student for poetry at the Northeast Ohio Master of Fine Arts program and she is the poetry editor for *Gordon Square Review*. She is the recipient of the 2016 Academy of American Poets University & College Poetry Prize for her poem "Kinsman." Her work has appeared in *A Race Anthology: Dispatches and Artifacts From a Segregated City, December, The Rumpus, jubilat, LitHub, One* and *The Offing*.